Path of Hope

Volume One

R. Darnell Smith

PATH OF HOPE

Volume One

By R. Darnell Smith

LPP Publishing™

Manchester, CT

Published by LPP Publishing, Manchester, CT

Lpppublishing1@Gmail.Com

Printed in the United States of America

First paperback edition September 2021
ISBN 978-1-7332643-5-8

D - *DETERMINED*

E - *EVOLVING*

D - *DESPITE*

I - *INADEQUATE*

C - *CIRCUMSTANCES*

A - *ALWAYS*

T - *TRUSTING*

I - *IN*

O - *OUR*

N - *NOBEL*

FATHER GOD!!!

I dedicate this book to the Prayer Warriors who constantly
PRAYED for me during my travels through the
wickedness I chose to follow.

I would list names, but that would be another book in itself.

So to those of you who know the words of prayer, please
continue to pray for me and mine.

~ R. Darnell Smith

September 17, 2004

Hey You,

My brilliant Big Brother. I just typed up some of your poems and they are really good. I will send the rest as I complete typing them. It's kind of hard being a wife and full time mother, but I am determined to get them to you as soon as possible. I am excited for you and praying that God continues to show you favor and bless you beyond your wildest dreams.

Some of your poems were a little sad, and I pray that you are all right. Please just be strong and Trust in the Lord with all of your Heart and lean not to your own understanding, In all of your ways acknowledge him and he will direct your path. Prayer does help, know that I am praying for you, missing you, and waiting for you to get out of there.

Sorry I don't write more, but believe me when I say not a day goes by that I don't think about you.

Here is the first chapter of my book. I hope you like it. You can keep it, and I will send more chapters when I get the chance.

I included $20.00 with this letter. Look out for it.

I will send more poems, another chapter, more money, pictures, and other stuff later.

Keep your head up!!

I Love You!!

Tasha

WHY I AM HERE!

SATAN THE BEAST, FOR YOUR SOUL HE'S OUT TO STEAL,
IF YOUR NOT BORNAGAIN, HE'LL SHOW YOU HELL IS REAL.
HAVE YOU FOUND SALVATION, IN JESUS YOUR SAVIOUR,
THERE'S LIFE IN THE BLOOD LISTEN LET ME TELL YA.
WITHOUT CHRIST, YOU DONT STAND A CHANCE,
WHEN SIN CATCHE'S UP WITH YOU, WITH THE DEVIL YOU'LL DANCE
I AM NOT HEAR TO HATE, LIKE THOSE WHO EXPIRED.
THOSE WITHOUT FAITH, ALL BURNED IN THE LAKE OF FIRE.
SIN SEPARATE'S US FROM GOD, AND THAT'S TO
MUCH FOR ME TO BEAR, TO OBEY THE WORD
OF GOD THIS IS WHY I AM HEAR.
FIRST I THOUGHT I WAS CURSED, AND LEFT IN A PLACE OF HATE
NOW I KNOW I AM HERE TO GET MYSELF STRAIGHT.
SO WHY I AM HERE, I MUST FORGET ABOUT MY PRIDE,
AND GAIN KNOWLEDGE, WISDOM, AND UNDERSTANDING, FROM DEEP INSIDE
I MUST RELEASE THOSE DEMON'S I USE TO POSESS
GIVE 100 % TO GOD, AND NOTHING LESS.
HOLE MY HEART, THAT WONT BE ENOUGH,
GIVING MY ALL MAKE'S IT EASY, WHEN IT GET'S ROUGH.
I WILL LISTEN CLOSE, TO MY HOLY VISITATION
AND TURN TO GOD, TO HELP BUILD A NEW NATION!

CONTENTS

ON THE MOUNTAIN   12

DREAMING   14

COME ABOARD   17

FORGIVE THOSE   18

YOU WERE THERE   20

BAD APPLE   24

HATE   25

SANITY   27

YES IT'S TRUE   30

DOWN AND OUT   32

JESUS ON THE MAINLINE   34

GUESS WHO'S COMING?   36

THIS MORNING   38

I AM A WORK IN PROGRESS   42

FOCUS   44

MY FATHER'S KINGDOM   46

I DESERVE IT   49

LIES AND THE TRUTH   51

GIVE GOD HIS GLORY   54

SOMEONE SAID   56

I LOVE YOU   58

SO GOOD TO ME   60

I DO KNOW   62

IN THE LAB AGAIN   65

TAKE IT TO HIM   67

OPEN DOORS   69

HUMBLE   71

I NEED YOU NOW   73

FATHER GOD   74

BROKE   76

THE PAST   78

DAY 26   80

<u>On The Mountain</u>

At some point
You must get away
So I traveled to the mountain
For some peace and time to pray

Many fell I've lost control
My life is in your hands and
I love the way you hold

Your grasp grips tight
With a clutch
This is why
I love you so much

At times I felt
You weren't here
As I look in the mirror
I can see you there

This journey
Is just the beginning
With you by my side
I know I am winning

For those with disbelief
I'll let them know
I am in the hands of the chief

Well now it's time
I lay down to rest
No worries
You are the best

My pillow is soft
Mattress is firm
This here is the first day
Of my term

It's ok I am with him
Good night to all
Good blessings Amen!

Dreaming

That sneaky snake
Came slithering through
In a dream
Through your stipes
I am clean

I sweated
Tossed and turned
Yet I had an advantage
Your mercy I've earned

Being obedient
Taken heed to your word
I may have had bad dreams
Yet my prayers were heard

When I rest
My thoughts take over
They took me to a place
Blessed by Jehovah
Jehovah Jireh
Lead me through the pain and sorrow
It was last night
Yet it brought me
Tomorrow

Yesterday is gone
So today I will cherish
Those still around
Those who did not parish

Giving thanks to God
God all mighty
His words and teachings
I hold highly

For those who go through
The suffering and pain
Please for God's sake
Give thanks
Through his name

We all have a number and a time
So until your number's called
Fall in line

Only one knows
When this shall happen

Some say mistake
Tragedy or accident

God only knows
The real way it went

So I thank you God
For all you have done
This is why I scream
Victory
With you
I've already
Won!

Come Aboard

At peace just me and the Lord
Praying and wishing you are aboard
I can't make no one
Join my journey
One thing I do know
Yes he is worthy
He'll come through
If you're dedicated
He's the reason
This season I made it
Don't get me wrong
There will be times and tests
I've learned to give it to him
He'll do the rest
It says let go and let God
While others hold on
I'll let him do his job
You see your faith must be strong
Yes your faith indeed
Must be like the mustard seed
I try not to use big words to deceive
Yet I know, faith is what you need
At peace just me and the Lord
When you see what he has done for me
You'll come aboard

Forgive Those

Lord forgive those
Who do not know
What it takes
For their spirit
To grow

Well it also
Took me some time
To learn we are the branches
You are the vine

Sometimes we stumble
At times
We even fall
Not knowing
This is when we call
Upon your name
Seeking forgiveness
Speaking out loud
Meaning repentance

Yes I've done this
Many times
I can feel your spirit
Saying your mine

Yes indeed
I am a child of God
To cherish and worship you
Is my job

Lord forgive those
Who do not know
Faith without works
Your spirit   19
Won't grow

You Were There

When I came to you Lord
You were there

"Hold up… Hold up"

When I thought
That no one cared
I walked around lost
You were there

I was timid and afraid
Life filled with fear
Thought there was no reason
For me to be here

Yes I had given up
Yet still you over flowed
My cup

Me not knowing claiming luck
Didn't understand
You wouldn't
Leave me stuck

I shall never forsake thee
How it is read
Found in the street
Flat line dead

For those who prayed
I give plenty thanks
Your words were true
Money in the bank

Though my account was empty
Stocks had no shares
Still Lord
You were there

Insufficient funds
Many thought it was over
It was you my Lord
No four leaf clover

Trials and tribulations
The bad and the good
I believed in you
You said you could

So as I look back in time
I can see clear as day
You made this happened
You did it your way

When I came to you Lord
You were there
Would put nothing on my plate
That I could not bare

So today with joy I praise your name
Nothing to me will ever be the same
What other people think
I really don't care
I was lost
Yet you were there

BAD APPLE

4/13/21

THEY SAY THERE IS A BAD APPLE
IN EVERY BUNCH
I FELT THAT WAY UNTILL I MET SUCH
A MIGHTY GOD IN WHICH I SERVE
THEY ALSO SAID YOU GET WHAT YOU DESERVE
WELL LET ME TELL YOU BOTH ARE TRUE
I LEARNED THROUGH DISOBEYING YOU
IT TOOK SOME WORK REPENTANCE AND PRAYER
I PUT ON MY SUIT OF ARMOR NO MORE FEAR
GOT MY FOCUS STRAIGHT NOW MY SIGHTS VERY CLEAR
OBEY YOUR TEACHINGS FOLLOW YOUR COMMANDS
HEAD HELD HIGH FEET PLANTED HOW I STAND
MANY FELT I WAS ROTTEN
YOUR WORDS THEY THOUGHT I HAD FOGOTTEN
WE WERE ALL BORN INTO SIN
YET THROUGH YOUR MERCY I CAN TRY AGAIN
SO NEVER GIVE UP KEEP YOUR FAITH AND (BELIEVE) BELIEF
I'VE GOTTEN WHAT I DESERVE A RELATIONSHIP WITH THE
CHIEF.
                BAD
THIS ONE APPLE DIDN'T SPOIL THE BUNCH
YOUR WORDS ARE LIKE FOOD I AM READY TO MUNCH
I GET FILLED WITH THE SPIRIT
STAY FULL THROUGH YOUR KNOWLEDGE
THAT THIS ONE BAD APPLE YOU DID ABOLISH
YES INDEED I AM UNDER YOU WING
A MIGHTY GOD KNOW AS THE KING
                    © DL

23

Bad Apple

They say there is a bad apple

In every bunch

I felt that way until I met such

A mighty God in which I serve

They also said you get what you deserve

Well let me tell you both are true

I learned through disobeying you

It took some work repentance and prayer

I put on my suite of armor no more fear

Got my focus straight and now my sight's very clear

Obey your teachings follow your commands

Head held high feet planted is how I stand

Many felt I was rotten

Your words they thought I had forgotten

We were all born into sin

Yet through your mercy I can try again

So never give up keep your faith and belief

I've gotten what I deserve a relationship with the chief

This one bad apple didn't spoil the bunch

Your words are like food I' am ready to munch

I get filled with the spirit

Stay full through your knowledge

That one bad apple you did not abolish

Yes indeed I am under your wing

A mighty God known as the King!

Hate

Lord why must one hate

Is it because they don't have their life straight

To me this makes no sense

They should take the dip their spirit needs a rinse

Some understand while others contemplate

They still have a chance it's not too late

Love thy brother as on loves them self

The rich Kingdom is where I wanna be

And nowhere else

Your word explains simple and clear

You may have hated me then but I would love to see you there

To reach this point I strive for that height

Through faith and works your name can be

In the lambs book of life

Though it's no easy task

No Corona 19 no need for the mask

Do people really understand?

This is not new just what you demand

You said you shall return

Is it eternal life or in the fire will you burn

You gave instruction for one to follow

For life today and a better tomorrow

Lord why must one hate

When they just can repent for past mistakes
Don't get me wrong I've traveled that road
As I got weak you carried the load
For this reason my life has changed
What I did was put it in your name
I struggle like everyone else do
When we meet I would like to hear I know you
Lord why one must hate
They better come to grips before it's too late

Sanity

Some say I am insane
But when it comes to my God
Brother man
I play no games

An eye for an eye
And a tooth for a tooth
Best believe me brother
He is the truth

Look at me… I'm living proof!

Well one day
I tried those pearly gates
But it wasn't my time
Must have been a mistake

I was doing wrong
Must have lost my attention
This day here
Yes I must mention

90% heat and a whole lot of booze
I had no respect for any of his rules

My temple I did abuse
He took my breath away
Because I was a fool

Someone was praying
I surely wasn't

Took four days for my return
A valuable lesson I did learn

D.O.A.
Yet he brought me through
Yes I am standing here
Looking at you
So never, ever tell me
What he can't do

Sanity
Yes I had lost my mind
Fortunately my father was kind
He's in the forgiving business
I was in Satan's clutches
Can I get a witness?

I am here through his grace and mercy

This is why I tell you

Yes he is worthy

So to all the nonbelievers

I will just say to you this

Spirituality is something

You should not resist

Sanity

Yes I was insane

Yet someone prayed for me

In God's name!

Yes It's True

True; you're my Lord and savior

Yes; I must watch my behavior

True; you're the first and the last

Yes' I must move on from my past

True; you said thy will be done

Yes; you're my father I am your son

True; victory is mine

Yes; your loves so divine

True; you grant forgiveness

Yes; I must believe this

True; you said I must have faith

Yes; I must keep myself straight

True; you said you shall return

Yes; some still haven't learned

True; you said the sky will break

Yes; this action you shall make

True; you said there will be trials and tribulations

Yes; you test through temptation

Yes it's true that I love you

True you keep the high sky blue

Yes you're the one who keeps on blessing

True through every blessing there's a lesson

Yes again you're watching my behavior

True you're my Lord and savior

Down And Out

While I was down and out
These words I would shout
Thank you Jesus without a doubt
You came to my rescue once again
You're not only my father but my best friend
I remember the time I crossed the line
Suffer and pain I did incline
Had to repent for the wrongs I've done
Had to pick up my sword and begin to run
In your direction I did travel
My feet kicked up rocks like a hot rod spits up gravel
The path was paved yet I strayed off course
So you had to show me with no remorse
While I was down and they counted me out
I came to my father the man with clout
The king of kings the first and the last
Blessings bestowed he will cast
You may be down but never give up
When you are thirsty he shall fill your cup
First you believe in your heart
Then you confess through your mouth
He's the overseer North East West and South
Yes you may be down and you know the reason
He will get you straight when it's your season

So do me a favor please repent and pray

Then you will receive your blessings

On your day!

Jesus On The Mainline

(Jesus on the mainline)
No robo call
You better answer
Or you may fall

(Jesus on the mainline)
Don't let it go to message
No answer means
You will learn a lesson

(Jesus on the mainline)
Your ringer better be on
You miss that call
Means you're doing wrong

(Jesus on the mainline)
You better click over
It's the real one Jehovah

(Jesus on the mainline)
Bet not have no block

(Jesus on the mainline)
Take your phone off lock

When Jesus is on the mainline

Answering is a must

On your currency it reads

In God we trust

So if your bill ain't paid you better do it fast

(Jesus on the mainline)

Don't let this call be your last

Guess Who's Coming?

Guess who's coming? The Son is coming
Guess who's coming? The Son is coming
If you're not ready you better start running
Because the Son is coming

He said one day he shall return
Is it the golden gates or will you burn?
His favor did you earn?
Will you here "I know you"
When it's your turn?
Or will you meet Satan
And his earn?

The winds will get fierce a break in the sky
His teachings did you try?
Or did you simply let the days go by?
Well your spirits rise after you die?

One thing I know to do
In this relationship I must stay true
I'm praying I did hope you did too

Wolves in sheep's clothing
The wicked turned wise

When I meet my maker

I will look him straight in his eyes

Hope I get chose as one of his guys!

False teachers will teach to lead you astray

Are you all good?

Come judgment day!

This Morning

When I woke this morning
I was feeling real good
He gave me life and breath
That I prayed he would

Every night before rest
Yes I pray
For my Father God
To give me another day

Well today was given
Through his strength
Now it's my responsibility
To travel the length

He giveth and also taketh away
So from his teaching
I shall not stray

I know it sounds easy
Yet it does get rough
I must understand
He will give me enough

As the road gets harder
 I must keep my focus
He giveth and he taketh
Like hocus pocus

When I woke this morning
Giving thanks first
Knowing if I follow his teaching
He will quench my thirst

My cup floweth over
With many blessings
Through that one on the throne
Whom I don't be testing

Giving thanks to God
For all he has done
Fulfilling my prayers
My Father God, number one!

"I AM A WORK IN PROGRESS"

WHEN I THINK I KNOW IT ALL
IVE LOST IT ALL
I AM A WORK IN PROGRESS
EVERY DAY I MUST LEARN
SOMETHING NEW
I AM A WORK IN PROGRESS
AN OPEN MIND TRUE I MUST HAVE
I AM A WORK IN PROGRESS
KNOWLEDGE OF SELF
KEEPS ME GOING
I AM A WORK IN PROGRESS
EACH ONE TEACH ONE
I AM A WORK IN PROGRESS
I MAY STUMBLE AND MAY FALL
I AM A WORK IN PROGRESS
WHEN I BELIEVE I AM RIGHT
JUST TO FIND OUT I AM WRONG
I AM A WORK IN PROGRESS
IVE STUDIED LONG THO FAILED THE TEST
I AM A WORK IN PROGRESS
THE FALL FROM THE TOP
IS QUICKER THAN THE RISE
I AM A WORK IN PROGRESS
YOU MUST CRAWL BEFORE YOU WALK
I AM A WORK IN PROGRESS
I WENT LEFT AND DIDNT GO RIGHT
I AM A WORK IN PROGRESS

40

HE WHO KNOWS IT ALL
KNOWS NOTHING AT ALL
WHAT GOES UP MUST COME DOWN
MANY MISTAKES IN LIFE IVE FOUND
THE EARTH ON ITS AXLES
SPIN'S ROUND AND ROUND
YOU CAME FROM AND MUST RETURN TO IT
THE GROUND
WILL YOUR SPIRITS RISE
OR ARE THEY HELL BOUND
MY FAITH IS MY FOUNDATION
MEANING I AM SOUND
MY LORD JESUS CHRIST
I AM GLAD THAT I FOUND
MY HUNT FOR SALVATION
IS LIKE A BLOOD HOUND
SOME SEE FAILURE
YET I SEE PROGRESS
AS LONG AS I REMEMBER
I AM A WORK IN PROGRESS

I Am A Work In Progress

When I think I know it all

I've lost it all

I am a work in progress

Every day I must learn

Something new

I am a work in progress

An open mind true I must have

I am a work in progress

Knowledge of self

Keeps me going

I am a work in progress

Each one teach one

I am a work in progress

I may stumble and I may fall

I am a work in progress

When I believe I am right

Just to find out I am wrong

I am a work in progress

I've studied long though failed the test

I am a work in progress

The fall from the top

Is quicker than the rise

I am a work in progress

You must crawl before you walk

I am a work in progress
I went left and didn't go right
I am a work in progress

He who knows it all
Knows nothing at all
What goes up must come down
Many mistakes in life I've found
The earth on its axis
Spins round and round
You came from and must return to it
The ground
Will your spirits rise?
Or are they hell bound
My faith is my foundation
Meaning I am sound
My Lord Jesus Christ
I am glad that I found
My hunt for salvation
Is like a blood hound
Some see failure
Yet I see progress
As long as I remember
I am a work in progress

Focus

Focus on righteousness
The battle is mine
You have already won
If you repent for your sins
Then your job is done

Negative thoughts lead to negative actions
Stop worrying remember your fractions

That devil is real he come in many forms
The wicked one you must not believe
He's very tricky out to deceive
God sees us he knows all of our needs

Do not be afraid little flock
Put your faith in God keep leaning on the rock
The Devil's madness he will stop

Gods kingdom your inheritance in heaven
Go to church listen to the Reverend

Every day when I wake up
I wake up with prayer
Praising your name

I may not see you

Yet I know you are there!

My Father's Kingdom

My father's kingdom paved in Gold
Are you spiritual?
Did you sale your soul?
I don't know about you
Yet I know about me
Every day I try to live sin free

Yes I try this I cannot deny
The devil has me running like a chicken
From the hot oil not ready to fry!

When my spirit is lifted
Up to those pearly gates
I don't know the date
One thing I do know
I won't be late!

Well if you know the date
And also the time
My father's kingdom
You will not find!

My Father's Kingdom is filled with riches
Boy oh boy I hope you don't miss this

Jesus died and rose
On the third day
He ascended to heaven
His resurrection
Yet before it he would say!

Surly I am with you
Through the spirit of truth
If you pray and repent
I will give you proof!

Peace and comfort
You shall inherit
Coming from me
Through the Holy Spirit
Can I get some praise?
Come on let me hear it!

Hallelujah, thank you my Father
If you can't big up his name
Then I won't bother

You see time is precious
He is getting near
Look at the world now

His story did you hear?

Have you red his story
If not I suggest that you do
All the things he said
Are coming true!

He said this would happen
Just as simple and plain
How many times a day
Do you mention his name?

Whether giving praise
Or asking in prayer
Jesus promised you
He would always
Be there!

I Deserve It

Through my heartache and pain
My ups and downs
I am still standing
Through the King with the crown
So when I rejoice
With big smiles and no frowns
Simply because he said
If you believe
I will not let you down

Believe is just one of the things you must do
Also work hard and confess this is true
Some beat around the bush
Claiming it ain't worth it
Boy, man, this feeling I got
Yes, I deserve it

I've worked hard
Changed a whole lot of ways
Man I see things different
Now a days

At times it may be sunny
Yet at times it will rain

These are those test days
To see if I can maintain

It is easy to love God
Yes this is true
Yet when thing go bad
You must just see it through

Please never give up
Thinking it ain't worth it
Stick your chest out
Stand strong
Claiming
I DESERVE IT!

Lies And The Truth

Some people speak truth
While some just run lies
Which one are you
Can you keep it real?
Or you out to despises

You have to be careful
Whom you entertain
Plain and simple
Everyone is not the same

The wolf in sheep's clothing
Claiming to be the one
Can you recognize,
The C.E.O from the bum?

Me, Myself I measure one's character
Actions speak louder than word
Can you hear me brah?

In these last days
You must learn the difference
Take your time
Slow down
Keep things specific

This here's no easy task
So weigh all your options
If you make the wrong choice
You better chose again
I hope you choose the forgiving God
My Father and Best Friend

Some people speak truth
While others run with lies
I pray your choice was not the wicked
But it was the wise.

GIVE GOD HIS GLORY

4/21/21

AT TIMES WHEN THINGS ARE GOOD
  YOU MUST TELL YOUR STORY
YOU EXPLAIN FACT FOR FACT
  WITH A BIG SMILE
YET NOT GIVING GOD HIS GLORY

IT HAPPENED LIKE THIS
  IT WENT LIKE THAT
DOWN TO EVERY DETAIL
  WORD FOR WORD
ACTIONS INCLUDED
  EXPLAINING HOW YOU PREVAILED

YOU HAVE A LOT LISTENERS
CROWDED AROUND GATHERED IN A CIRCLE
SHOWING THEM HOW YOU DEFENDED YOURSELF
FROM SOMEONE OUT TO HURT YOU

THEY WERE BIG VERY ~~STRON~~ STRONG
  THREW BLOWS LIKE GEORGE FORMAN
THE MAIN THING YOU LEFT OUT
  IN YOUR OUTLANDISH STORY
THAT YOU TOOK ALL THE CREDIT
  YET NEVER GAVE GOD HIS GLORY.

THE MORAL OF THE POEM
  IS TO TELL YOU THIS
WITH OUT YOUR LORD AND SAVIOUR
  THIS ENCOUNTER COULD'NT ~~EXES~~ EXSIST
SO THE NEXT TIME YOU COME ARROUND
  WITH SITUATIONS WHICH MAY BORE ME
I WILL NOT LEND AN EAR
UNLESS YOU GIVE GOD HIS GLORY !

Give God His Glory

At times when things are good
You must tell your story
You explain fact for fact
With a big smile
Yet not giving God his glory

It happened like this
It went like that
Down to every detail
Word for word
Actions included
Explaining how you prevailed

You have a lot of listeners
Crowded around gathered in a circle
Showing them how you defended yourself
From someone out to hurt you

They were big very strong
Threw blows like George Foreman
The main thing you left out
In your outlandish story
That you took all the credit
Yet never gave God his glory

The moral of the poem
Is to tell you this
Without your Lord and Savior
This encounter couldn't exist
So the next time you come around
With situations which may bore me
I will not lend an ear
Unless you give God his glory

Someone Said

Someone said

God look after babies and fools

Many they live by these rules

They cut up and then cry

Thinking this is the way to get by

God knows you better than yourself

So you better be careful

Stop your conning and bluffing

Take it from me he will show you something

Don't get me wrong

God loves all of his children

Whether sane or not

Yet all that conniving stuff

He will bring to a stop

He knows your intentions

Your motives and schemes

Do you really understand

The meaning of bad dreams

You better take heed to the signal

And slow yourself down

When you meet your destiny

Is it heaven or hell bound?

Keep playing games trying to be slick

Don't be that one in a million

The one not being picked

I will share with you something

In which I had to do

Change my life around

Stop living through lies

And live life true

I Love You

God I love you
This is true
You turn my gloomy days
Bright sunny blue
You can calm the winds
To a gentle breeze
It's you that I mention
After someone has a sneeze

You grant birth
Yet cancel life
Those unworthy of your sacrifice

Your realm brings heat
From the hot sun
Soft snow you let fall
For some winter fun

You gave wings to birds
To gain flight
Who… Who… goes the owl at night
You made Leo the lion
King of the jungle
You also bring thunder
In the storms to rumble

I can go on about all you created

It's you that I mention

When I think of how I made it

God I love you

This is true

For those who don't share my love for God

I suggest that you do!

So Good To Me

Lord you have been so good to me

I mention your name so much

It's like it's WE

I do believe that's the way it should be

Before I had doubts

I mean second guessing

Now I really know I am a blessing

At times I would take things for granted

Not realizing I was a seed you planted

I would block the sun and shun the water

People these days call me a hoarder

Yeah I have plenty of your stuff

Yet when it comes to you

I could never get enough

Don't get me wrong my ears are wide open

Telescopic lens how I be scoping

Always seeking for something new

When I think I know it all

Then my time is through

So basically I will keep an open mind

Daily expecting miracles

From the one divine

Lord you have been so good to me

You have broken the yoke

Set me free

There is no one greater than thee

Lord, Lord, Let it be!

I Do Know

Yes I do know
His name is Jesus
He gave breath
To me and you

He is coming back
He's mine and yours
Obey his word
Are your chores

He's the King of Kings
Yes indeed
We are his seeds
Read the Bible
And take heed
He will give you
All you need!

Faith in God
Is for me and you
Keep faith in God
He'll come through!

SONG   4/7/21

WHY DO T KNOW   BRE
YES I DO   Z
YOU DONT KNOW   BRE
YES I DO   Z

YOU DONT KNOW   Z
YES I DO   BRE
YOU DONT KNOW   Z
YES I DO   BRE

WELL WHAT'S HIS NAME   BRE
    JESUS   Z
WELL WHA'S HIS NAME   BRE
    JESUS   Z
WHAT DID HE DO   Z
HE GAVE BREATH TO YOU   BRE
WHAT DID HE DO   Z
HE GAVE BREATH TO YOU BRE
WELL IS HE COMMING BACK   BRE
YES HE HIS   Z
WELL IS HE COMMING BACK   BRE
YES HE HIS   Z
HE'S MINE AND YOURS   } BOTH
HE'S MINE AND YOURS
WELL WHAT ARE YOUR CHORESS Z
OBEY HIS WORD   BRE   (CR)
WELL WHAT WHAT ARE YOUR CHORESS Z
OBEY HIS WORD   BRE

63

IS HE'S THE KING OF KING'S   BRE

YES INDEED   Z

IS HE THE KING OF KING'S   BRE

YES IN DEED   Z

WE ARE HIS SEED'S } BOTH

WE ARE HIS SEED'S }

READ YOUR BIBLE } BRE

AND TAKE HEED

HE WILL GIVE YOU } Z

ALL YOU NEED

YOU DONT KNOW   BRE

YES I DO   Z

YOU DONT KNOW   BRE

YES I DO   Z

FAITH IN GOD   } BOTH

IS FOR   }

ME AND YOU

EM

KEEP FAITH IN GOD

CAUSE   } BOTH

HE'LL COME THROUGH

I DO KNOW

HIS NAME IS, JESUS

HE GAVE BREATH TO ME AND YOU

HE'S COMMING BACK, HE'S MINE AND YOURS

SO OBEY ~~THE~~ HIS WORD, DO YOUR CHORE'S

KEEP FAITH IN GOD   CR

TH KING OF KING'S

WILL COME THROUGH

In The Lab Again

It's me in the lab again

My daily conversations with my best friend

The only one who never let me down

I may have strayed away

Yet he brought me back around

The world is very tricky

It offers many different things

Things I took advantage of

Money girls liquor drugs strife

The fast life

Thought I was the man

The devil he had a plan

One day he would hold me

By my side he would stand

Steady throwing shade

A mad man he had made

He thought he had won

In the street I laid

Upon prayer request

My friend who is the best

Came to my rescue

So I am here to confess

I know I did you wrong

Kicked you to the curb

For my disobedience

A lesson I did learn

Good friends are really hard to find

Man oh man I am glad that you are mine

With you having my back

I am prepared for his attack

Four words I use when I feel the slack

It goes like this and the devil, he be hating

I simply speak it out

STAND BEHIND ME SATAN!

Take it to Him

There is no problem

He cannot mend

All you must do is

Take it to him

Caught up in confusion

Trapped in turmoil

Ready to burst wide open

Temperatures ready to boil

Take it to him

The one who stays loyal

Heading in the wrong direction

Things are looking dim

Sign reads dead end as you come around the bend

All you must do is take it to him

Wake up in the morning

Your shower water doesn't get hot

Going to be late for work yet

This time you cannot

Boss already gave you your last shot

Don't know what to do

You're hanging on a limb

Only one thing to do

Take it to him

Times get rough things can be hectic

For these reasons he's resurrected

Fully qualified yet you were rejected

Nothing left to do just must respect it

The wrong candidate was just elected

Everything's going wrong

You got a package in the mail

Not the one you selected

Your life is in shambles

Yet you must accept it

Gave your wife a ring

Filled with glass

When she wanted a GEM

Look at yourself in the mirror

Then say

I will leave it all

To him

Open doors

Doors must close in order for others to open
So I keep my focus I am steady scoping
I have given up on wishing and hoping

I'll continue to speak it into existence
With my faith and works he'll hold no resistance
It may take some time I'll go the distance

I understand it will not happen overnight
Through repentance and prayer I am ready to fight
I have on my suit of armor sword in my clutch
My defense mechanism the devil can't touch

Yes I understand that he'll never quit
This is why I train hard to deal with it
Don't get me wrong the enemy is relentless
No sleeping on my travels cannot afford this

In order for doors to open many must close
For the bad times I've been through
I am thankful for those
As I journey through all the trials and tribulations
A better life I'll be facing
When this happens I'll be on my way
To hear I know you son come judgment day

Again many doors must close for others to open

So as I approach those gates my sword I'll be toting

Praising God for the good and the bad

Getting there isn't easy and no I ain't mad

I just use the right things in which I have

Many times and things made me sad

Look upon the smile on my face

You can see I am glad

Humble

Today Lord I come to you humble
I've overreacted in situations
Which caused me to stumble
Took things the wrong way
I should have been serious
Yet I wanted to play

Time occurs when you must give it your all
Will you stand upright and firm or shall you fall
Are you prepared for what lies ahead?
Or will you cry your eyes bloodshot red
Wipe your tears and clean up your act
Life is not fiction life is a fact

As you grow you must keep an open mind
Ready to accept that everyone will not treat you kind
The good and the bad is what you'll find
Can you distinguish one from another?
As you love yourself you must love thy brother
This gets twisted by many who hate
Those non-believers who steady debate

Your life is your own filled with many choices
Be careful in your head you'll hear many voices

Telling you this and telling you that
Again life is not fiction life is real fact

So do your best live life to the fullest
Except no wrong teaching the devil he pulls this
Everything that glitters is not gold
Know his story and how it was told
The real way in which it unfolds
Know for yourself so you will not stumble
To live a sin free life true and humble

I Need You Now

Come to me Lord I need you now
My hands are folded on my knees I bow
Asking for mercy and your grace
My better life leaves a terrible taste
I am running in circles thinking I am winning the race

I stumbled over hurdles through choices of mine
I am still running yet see no finish line
Could it be I chose the wrong course?
I went my way didn't check the source
The path I've chosen must have been wrong
So I've been running my whole life long

Well I'll keep moving
Searching for your affection
When you're ready
You will give me the direction
This time I will listen to you
Then claim first place
And your blessings too

Father God

Father God your mercy is unmatchable

Yet I strayed and became an attachable

I switched sides which was the wrong thing to do

Now here I stand trying to explain to you

As I tried to give excuses and all the reasons

Why I committed such a thing as treason

The devil offered me more though it may have seemed

His worldly ways was a good scheme

The bright lights fast cars and cash

I believed in limelight, things moving fast

I thought it was the best thing, thought it would last

Someone was praying in my best interest

Simply because you put his trickery to rest

Now here I stand before you, ready to confess

Tears in my eyes because I settled for less

I pray I didn't bring upon you too much stress

Looking back on how this all went down

He had me starring in his circus playing a clown

I had the lead role nominated for an Oscar

Little did I know my spirit did not prosper

The director should have been you yet I chose an impostor

Now that you've come for the takeover and

Changed the scene, cancelled out that devil

And all of his team

Brought in your crew and a whole new cast,

Slow me down, brought me back to the past

Back when I had morals and values

Someone prayed for me that I would have you

That Oscar looked good with all that shine

Yet I'd rather have you, you're so divine

The moral of the story is simply this

If you trust in father God, you will continue to exist

Broke

I may be broke in wealth broke in health

Broke in transportation so I stay to myself

Many judge by worldly possessions

Listen closely, are you broke from confessions?

How much time do you spend with the Lord?

This conversation can you afford?

Do you bring it to him

When your worldly bright gems, turn real dim?

Should I explain how one came to glory

Did you take time yourself to read his story?

I know as a kid you went to service

Now as an adult do you do service?

You have all your riches, cars and homes

Do you acknowledge the king on the throne?

I ain't talking about LeBron James

Talking about the poor king who came to fame

Did you understand what it took?

How many days a week do you open his book?

Well times are different now

All you have to do is Google

When it comes time well he say he knew you know lie you

just can't read you must also live

By the directions this king gives

Yes there are some instructions

Not following those is self-destruction

For me how he changed my life to send free

Sin free not send free forget about the army

If you're in his armed forces you can be

All you can be and all he asks is to live like me

Not me, him of course - I hope that little dip

Didn't throw you off course

A little dip yes you must take

It cleanses your soul then you repent for mistakes

Basically I gave you a taste

If you're not committed your time you will waste

See I may be broke with finance

Broke with health but when it comes to faith I have much
wealth

Here today gone tomorrow

Tell me when it's gone will you live in sorrow

Time is getting short he shall return

Everlasting life or are you chicken

In the fire that burns

The Past

As I sit back and think of the past

Giving thanks to our father through him I can last

Many times I've lived on the edge

Doing unthinkable things just for a blast

Worrying my mom's an also my pops

They both came to me and said this has to stop

Me being the one who I was

Paid no attention seeking the buzz

It got so bad I went so far

Front page of the paper I made the news I was a star

In and out of jail in prison to

What's that saying? It do what it do

I guess I was searching for attention

How I got notice I was sent to prison

What will I do little old me

I was on a bus with guys three times me

He said asking you shall receive

Going somewhere if I wanted to go I could not leave

It do what it do, do you remember that line?

5 feet 100 pounds heading to the Penn

Now I am in a bind

All I can do is surrender no more debate

I must leave it to God and have a whole lot of faith

Timid and nervous on my arrival

No muscle so I leaned on the rock for my survival

I began to write which was my daily routine

This was my only way to escape this real living dream

You lay locked in a room 100 men

I knew no one, had no friend

Still I had one weapon in which I brought aboard

With faith and my weapon - the Bible

Which is also named a sword

Before I got sentence I did take the dip

I finally listened to my parents before the trip

I'm standing here today with not a broken limb

What I did was I left it to him

I seen many things that's not good to mention

Instead of looking for, I paid attention

Still I have a long way to go

Understanding and being obedient

Is how your spirit will grow

Am I still looking for that type of life?

The answer is no

I'd rather live my life out surrounded by Godly men

This way I know I will always have a friend

Day 26

Day 26 times getting short
I've been doing things
To strengthen my Forte
You see this journey
Is coming to an end
My distant relationship
I had to mend

Many days and many nights
One on one talks
Has gotten me right
Before this journey
I would only call when in distress
Now I call when I wake
And before I rest
No one else
Could clean up my mess

I was living life wrong
Many I did without hesitation
Simple and plain
It was a failure of communication

Well I've broke out
Of my rebellious ways

Things are looking a whole lot better nowadays

I still suffer meaning I need more work
I need to gain trust back
From people I've hurt

It's gonna take time
And a whole lot of forgiveness
Yet I must stay humble
And handle my business

Some have forgiven me
While others hold the grudge
I must keep on moving
And leave it to the man above

He holds my faith
Knows the outcome
Before it happens
So I'll trust in his word
When it's done
I'll start clapping

Clapping that sound of relief
Knowing I've done the right thing
Confirmation from the chief

I know you have heard the saying
here today gone tomorrow, this is
why I live everyday in joy no time
for sorrow.
For you Lord I must live, also I must
die, While here on earth your truth
shall set me free, taken those word
from Maya Angelou "still I rise".
You were crucified, beat even nailed to
the Cross for all the non-believers they
took a loss, Yet they celebrated in joy
partyed with cheer, until 3 day's later
you were'nt there. O what a miricel
when your tomb was opened, in
the nay-sayers were schocked
an empty tomb covered with rocks.
Well if you don't know the story how
one came to glory, read the WORD
and learn the story. Born by a
miricel conception, to lead the
multitudes, who would follow HIS
progressions. Some may believe while
others shall doubt
I will believe in my heart
and confess through my mouth.
Its never too late to be born
again just try Jesus what a
wonderful Friend!

To Lorenzo
May God continue to bless you and yours
"Rick"